Learning From La Jolla

Robert Venturi Remakes
a Museum in the
Precinct of Irving Gill

Hugh M. Davies and Anne Farrell
Essay by Robert Venturi
Interview with Robert Venturi
by Hugh M. Davies and Ronald J. Onorato

This book was published by the Museum of Contemporary Art,
San Diego as part of a year's celebration of the expanded and renovated
La Jolla building. It was made possible by the generous support of
Lela (Jackie) and Rea Axline, and other donors to the Museum's 50th
Anniversary Campaign.

Designed by Richard P. Burritt
Printed by Precision Litho, San Diego,
in an edition of 3,750

ISBN 0-934418-47-0 (paper)
ISBN 0-934418-48-9 (cloth)
Library of Congress Catalogue Card Number 96-79507

Paperback edition available through
D.A.P./Distributed Art Publishers
636 Broadway, 12th Floor
New York, NY 10012
Tel: (212) 473-5119   Fax: (212) 673-2887

Cover photograph: © Timothy Hursley
Title page: Detail of front arched entry, Scripps House, c. 1930s

Contents

Acknowledgments

The publication of this book helps commemorate the 1996 reopening of the Museum of Contemporary Art, San Diego, after renovation and expansion of its La Jolla site. MCA is now one museum with two locations: the new La Jolla building and MCA Downtown, completed and opened in 1993. My first and most heartfelt expressions of gratitude go to the Museum's Board of Trustees and the generous benefactors who made both Museum expansion projects possible.

This book came about because we felt it important to make a permanent record of the rich lore of this place. Our research unearthed some wonderful early photographs, unpublished reminiscences by Museum founder Samuel Weston, and newspaper articles and archival materials at the La Jolla Historical Society (LJHS). We acknowledge LJHS Archivist Sandra Zarcades, and the Society's president, Pat Schaelchlin, for their generous help and especially for Pat's book on La Jolla[1]. Our work was aided immeasurably by Joy Wolf, who transcribed tapes of the Venturi interview in her capacity as volunteer chairwoman of the Museum's Oral History Committee, and other volunteers who have made sure that our historical records are in order and accessible.

We are grateful to Ellen Revelle Eckis, who was born in 1910 in the guest house next-door to her aunt, Ellen Browning Scripps. Mrs. Eckis graciously reviewed the historical facts and added a number of important pieces of information about her family, the home and the neighborhood she knew as a child and young woman. Architect Robert Mosher shared with us his photographic archive as well as reminiscences of his long history with this Museum from its earliest days, and we are grateful for his valuable contributions. I want to acknowledge the work of our former Senior Curator, Ronald J. Onorato, who in his time at MCA (1985-88) was instrumental in the selection of Venturi, Scott Brown and Associates, and who joined me in conducting the interview of Mr. Venturi in 1994. We must also acknowledge the late Bruce Kamerling, former curator at the San Diego Historical Society. Bruce spent his professional life studying the architects and artists of San Diego's past, and we are in his debt for the scholarly contribution he made to understanding and appreciating the work of Irving Gill. A great regret is that Bruce did not live to see the final restoration of the Scripps House, as he was our "source" for so many of the historic details and restoration decisions made early on in the project.

The handsome look of this publication is thanks to Richard Burritt, designer of the myriad of materials associated with the Museum's inauguration. Rick worked tirelessly with MCA's former Curator, Lynda Forsha, who coordinated all graphic and interior design for the La Jolla reopening and helped realize a number of important publications subsequent to the reopening, including this one. For editorial assistance, we are especially grateful to John Farrell, as well as to Julie Dunn, Christian Kleinbub, and Hilary Snow.

Associate Director Charles Castle skillfully oversaw the La Jolla construction project, and we are thankful for the enormous time and energy he devoted to it over six years. Museum Manager Tom Flowers, who in his twenty-two years at MCA has seen this building through several incarnations, was instrumental to the project. All members of the Museum's curatorial, administrative and development staff in one way or another contributed to ambitious construction project and the Museum's successful reopening. The staff is listed in the back of the book, but for their help in assembling this book, I would particularly like to thank Development staff members Synthia Malina, Jini Bernstein, Jessica O'Dwyer, and former staff member Gwen Hollister, and our Librarian Virginia Abblitt and Registrar Mary Johnson. Special thanks goes to my friend and colleague of ten years, Anne Farrell.

Our title plays on that of the seminal publication, *Learning from Las Vegas*,[2] the authors of which also happen to be our architects, the brilliant Robert Venturi and Denise Scott Brown. More than a decade ago, we first began discussions with them regarding this project. The fruits of their work, and ours, are even more gratifying because of the commitment and tenacity of everyone involved. In the process, we have all "learned from La Jolla" and created a building that incorporates the history of this site, its previous owner Ellen Browning Scripps, and its previous architects Irving Gill and Robert Mosher, as well as the larger context of our Gill-designed neighborhood and our exquisite oceanfront locale. Words are inadequate to express my thanks and gratitude to Bob and Denise for sticking with us and bringing such passion and architectural genius to our project.

Hugh M. Davies, Director

The Scripps House, c. 1930

The Scripps House:
Overlooking the Pacific in La Jolla

In 1957, *Architectural Record* magazine polled a large number of architects and came up with a list of the fifty most important houses in America since 1850.[3] On that list, tied for ninth place, was the Art Center of La Jolla at 700 Prospect Street. Originally called the Scripps House, it was designed in 1916 by Irving Gill[4] for Ellen Browning Scripps.

In that article, it acknowledged Gill as "one of the unsung pioneers of modern architecture, and one of the most isolated. During the second decade of the century, he produced in the San Diego region buildings of an amazing modernity. Smooth skinned, geometric, with large sheets of plate glass and strip windows, they are the antithesis of the baroque fantasies of Maybeck or the inspired carpentry of the Greene brothers, his leading California contemporaries. Indeed, they seem entirely apart from the Richardson-Sullivan-Wright mainstream of American modernism. If his remote ancestor was Claude-Nicolas Ledoux in the 1790s, his most obvious descendent is the European 'International Style' of the twenties and thirties. With a style of ruthless elegance, Gill seems a sort of early Corbusier anchored to the ground."[5]

The clean lines and balanced volumes of the Scripps House reflected Gill's desire to "... get back to the source of all architectural strength – the straight line, the arch, the cube, and the circle."[6] In an article published in *The Craftsman* the same year the Scripps House was finished, Gill said: "The arch is one of our most imposing, most picturesque and graceful architectural features. Its power of creating beauty is unquestionable." Further in that same article, he stated: "There is something very restful and satisfying to my mind in the simple cube house with creamy walls, sheer and plain, rising boldly into the sky, unrelieved by cornices or roof overhangs ... I like the bare honesty of these houses, the childlike frankness and chaste simplicity of them."[7]

One of the most important critics and writers on California architecture, Esther McCoy, was a passionate admirer of Irving Gill. She described how his style "...grew out of what he found in Southern California. He added elements that were missing, and produced an architecture as un-insistent as the change of seasons. It was an architecture of modesty, and repetition. The elements he repeated were those which his perceptive eye recognized as good; they had been tried and tried again until they reached the ideal of appropriateness. Gill was a conservator of the past, building always for the present, in new materials, with new methods evolved through arduous trial and error."[8] Another dominant scholar of California architectural history, David Gebhard, also greatly admired the work of Irving Gill, but lamented the fact that he "was almost a prophet without honor in his own country ... what happened to most of his buildings forms a sorry chapter in the history of the destruction of the usable past."[9]

Gill's Scripps House, perhaps above all his other buildings, has the singular distinction of reflecting regional American history (the missions, the pueblos) while at the same time precursing what twenty years later would be the predominant architectural language around the world: the International Style. In 1959, extensive modifications and renovations to the building largely obscured the Scripps House facade and the hand of Irving

Ellen Browning Scripps, at the time of her graduation from Knox College, Illinois, c. 1859

Gill on 700 Prospect Street. But the building's impact has lingered in architectural history books and people's memories for nearly forty years.

The Legendary Miss Scripps

Born in London in 1836, at Number 13 South Moulton Street, Ellen Browning Scripps was the daughter of James Mogg Scripps and Ellen Mary Saunders Scripps.[10] After the death of both Ellen's mother and step-mother, James Scripps and his large family emigrated to Illinois in 1844, where he remarried, ran a farm, and struggled to support his still-growing family (five more children were born in the U.S.). After high school, Ellen taught school and saved money so that she could attend Knox College in Illinois, where she graduated in 1859 at the age of twenty-three – one of the first women college graduates in the United States.

Ellen's brothers James and George had launched the Detroit *Tribune*, where she was a proofreader in 1867; later they were joined by E.W. Scripps, Ellen's half-brother. After a fire closed down the *Tribune,* resulting in a handsome insurance settlement, James, E.W., and Ellen

A vintage postcard image of the original seaside "cottage" of Ellen Scripps, a local landmark

The wood-frame house sat on a bluff overlooking the rocky shore

A scrap-book page showed the front of "South Moulton Villa," with an inset of the ocean view seen from the back of the house c. 1900

decided to start a new, more modern paper in 1873. For their Detroit *Evening News*, Ellen headed the copy desk and wrote a weekly column known by the staff as "Miss Ellen's Miscellany." Her column for the *Evening News* continued as she traveled in Europe from 1881 to 1883. Other family members sold their farms and put money into the venture, with Ellen serving as investor, consultant and close confidante to her by-then very successful step-brother, E.W. Scripps.

Miss Scripps was actively involved in many of the progressive social and political movements of the late nineteenth century – labor unions, temperance societies, educational reform, women's suffrage – and had wide interests and intellectual curiosity. She never married, but would often go to live with family members for a period of time or travel to exotic places with friends or family. The Scripps newspaper business continued to grow and prosper, although eventually family feuds divided the huge fortune into many branches. Throughout those disputes and over their lifetimes, E.W. and Ellen remained close.

In 1890, E.W.'s ill health drove him to Southern California in search of warm weather and perhaps some distance from the family rancor. He settled on some two thousand acres north of the city of San Diego, where he built an estate he called "Rancho Miramar." Shortly thereafter, he bought the San Diego *Sun*, a paper that later became the San Diego *Tribune*.

In 1897, at the age of sixty-one, Ellen was by then independently wealthy and she, too, moved West, in part to be near her beloved half-brother. She established her home in the small town of La Jolla (population: not quite 100), where she found a spectacular oceanfront bluff site on Prospect Street. There, she built an impressive two-story wood-frame house that her sister, Virginia, named "South Moulton Villa" in honor of the London street where Ellen was born.

Throughout the rest of her life, Ellen Browning Scripps was active in supporting causes in her adopted home town. Much of her fortune went to projects that benefited the health and welfare of children and young people. Among

Irving Gill, c. 1905

The garden and ocean view from the Scripps House "sun parlor"

them were the La Jolla Children's Playground (now called the Recreation Center), the La Jolla Library, the La Jolla Woman's Club, the La Jolla High School Athletic Field, the San Diego Zoo, Scripps Memorial Hospital, and Scripps Clinic. She was the founder of Scripps College in Claremont, and was the patron of other educational establishments including the Scripps Institution of Oceanography in La Jolla (now part of the University of California, San Diego) and her alma mater, Knox College. She supported all of the churches of La Jolla as well as funding the tower and chimes at St. James By-The-Sea Episcopal Church across the street from her home. Writing in 1899 on the future of La Jolla, Miss Scripps described her adopted community: "For here the poet will find his inspiration, the teacher his lessons. Here the artist shall realize his dream, the weary and suffering shall find rest and solace, and every soul shall be satisfied."

The wood-frame seaside "cottage" of Ellen Scripps, located at the south end of Prospect Street, commanded a view for miles around. It was one of the most distinctive buildings in the sparsely populated village fifteen miles north of the city of San Diego, due west from E.W.'s "Miramar" acreage. Around the turn of the century, La Jolla, with its beautiful beaches and temperate climate, became a haven for wealthy East Coast and Midwest expatriates. Avant-garde artists, writers, and eccentrics often stayed for months at a time at Anna Held's famous "Green Dragon Colony" of cottages located on Coast Boulevard, just north of Miss Scripps'.

South Moulton Villa, overlooking the rocky shore, was built in 1897 by Thorpe, Kennedy & Johnson (responsible for many of La Jolla's earliest buildings). It had a prominent cupola and lush formal garden originally designed by landscape artist Kate Sessions[11] who created many of San Diego's most beautiful gardens. The meandering garden facing Coast Boulevard was well known and much admired. Ellen Scripps and her gardeners were constantly moving plants and trees from one place to another, which changed the vistas from the windows of the house. One of Miss Scripps' ten gardeners, who had been dismissed from service, reputedly set fire to the wooden South Moulton Villa, presumably in an act of revenge. It burned to the ground in 1915. At the age of seventy-nine, Ellen Scripps, very forward-thinking for her day (as well as practical), engaged the talented forty-five-year-old San Diego architect Irving Gill to rebuild her house on the same lot. In the course of just one year, he designed and built for her a startlingly modern building, one of the first to use concrete and stucco. Not coincidentally, it was far more fireproof than its predecessor. His modernist structure on Prospect Street, completed in 1916, was also named South Moulton Villa by Miss Scripps, but later came to be called by others the "Scripps House."

Irving Gill explained his design philosophy in his 1916 article in *The Craftsman*,[12] that was prefaced by a quote: "An artist is known rather by what he omits." Gill went on to say: "If we, the architects of the West, wish to do great and lasting work, we must dare to be simple, must have the courage to fling aside every device that distracts the eye from structural beauty, must break through convention and get down to fundamental truths. ... I believe if we continually think more of line, proportion, light and shade, we will reach greater skill in understanding them, and a greater appreciation and understanding of their power and beauty." His Scripps House more than fulfilled this belief, and was exceptional in its appreciation of space, light, and function. Those values, captured in a building of straightforward simplicity and beauty, elevated the residence to one of the finest examples of American residential design in the twentieth century.

From Scripps House to Art Center

Ellen Scripps died in 1932 at the age of ninety-six. The Ellen B. Scripps Estate divided the large property into a number of parcels and eventually sold all but the parcel containing the house, which came into the possession of neighboring Scripps Hospital. In Depression-era San Diego, the house remained vacant until November 1940, when a group of artists asked the trustees of the hospital if

(left) Miss Scripps standing at her back door; the "sun parlor" with its large windows surmounted the *porte-cochère* at the north of the site

(below) A view of the Scripps House from Prospect Street (the guest cottage to the right was later relocated to another lot)

9

Architect Robert Mosher standing at the northwest corner of the Art Center he redesigned in 1951

they could use the empty building for an exhibit of their work. The showing coincided with President Franklin D. Roosevelt's declaration of National Art Week, which he proclaimed with the slogan "American Art in Every American Home." The exhibition in Miss Scripps' house was so successful that it was followed by several others; and in 1941, a group of community leaders incorporated "The Art Center in La Jolla" as a private, nonprofit organization. The first Board of Trustees purchased the house from Scripps Hospital for the grand sum of $10,450, with additional donations from the community secured for improvements to the buildings as well to establish an operating endowment of $10,000.

An article in the *La Jolla Journal* in 1941 enumerated estimated operating expenses for the new Art Center's first year. According to the President of the Board, Dr. William Thompson, and the head of the fund raising committee, Gordon Gray, their requirements were: "$120, Heat; $72, Light; $200, Caretaker; $1,200, Curator; $100, Fire Insurance; $108, Freight Charges; $100, Postage and Incidentals; and $600, Taxes. There will, of course, be revenue. Memberships of various classifications will be

sold. Auctions will be held and rentals coming in. It is planned to have teas, lectures and similar public functions for which the Center is admirably adapted. A nominal admission will be charged. Conservative estimates show an annual revenue of around $3,200."[13] Thanks to the hard work of Mr. Gray, Mr. Thompson and other volunteers, an additional $4,000 was raised that first year to ensure the operations of the fledgling organization.

The original Art Center used the rooms of the house as galleries and featured changing exhibitions of local artists selected by the first Curator Elsie Taft and first Director Freda Klapp. Early Boards of Trustees sat around Miss Scripps' dining room table and grappled with finances to keep the venture afloat. In September 1943, during World War II, the building was briefly occupied by the U.S. Army; but in March 1944 the Art Center resumed operations. Over the next nine years, the original property purchased from Scripps Hospital was augmented with a gift of oceanfront land from Mrs. Alma Doerge Skinner, and additional purchases of adjacent property, including Miss Scripps' former guest cottage to the north (that became the Children's Art Center) and the cottage to the south that had been the Scripps library.

By 1950, San Diego architects Robert Mosher and Roy Drew of the firm Mosher & Drew[14] were commissioned by the Art Center's President Gordon Gray to modify the structure. It reopened in 1951. Former living areas were rearranged and modified into more formal main galleries on the ground floor, one of which later became the Lynn G. Fayman Gallery in honor of Mr. Fayman's long devotion to the Museum. A gallery named for benefactor Charles F. Meyer was installed at the north side, and the rear lower *porte-cochère* was enclosed and converted to usable space for storage and classrooms. Second-floor bedrooms became offices and library in a skillful design that made the building much more suitable as a community art center. Mr. Mosher later said of his 1950 renovation, "I felt that my responsibility was to try to be thoughtful of the simplicity and the spirit of Gill's work, for which we had great admiration."[15]

(below and right background) The Art Center under renovation

SAN DIEGO UNION: SUNDAY MORNING, JULY 20, 1941

La Jollans to House Paintings in Noted Building

Home of the late Miss Ellen Browning Scripps at La Jolla overlooking the ocean is to become the permanent home of the La Jolla Art Center whose museum has been occupying the building for years.

CHILDREN'S ART CENTER

ART CENTER

(above right) The north cottage was used as a children's art center until its relocation in the late 1950s

(below right) Rear view of the Art Center, following its first renovation

Transformations

From the Art Center to the La Jolla Museum of Art

Over the next decade, the Art Center's audience and services outgrew its facilities. Plans were launched in 1959 for a new auditorium and other modifications. For the renovations, Mosher & Drew were again enlisted by Gordon Gray, and the modified building reopened on January 9, 1960, after an $800,000 construction project. A new 500-seat auditorium named in honor of benefactor Franklin P. Sherwood was built on the site of the former Scripps library cottage to the south (which was demolished), while the northern guest cottage was moved intact to another site on a bluff in La Jolla. In its place, Mosher designed a new driveway, parking lot, and loading dock. Improvements included additional exhibition galleries and office space, and an outdoor sunken "sculpture court" at the heart of the building on the eastern side.

It was during this 1959-60 renovation that Irving Gill's Scripps House facade was concealed and a new, more "modern" aesthetic of concrete block and colonnades appeared on Prospect Street. The original fenestration was bricked in and Gill's distinctive signature arched entry was removed. Also removed were the stately palms that had been planted in front of Ellen Browning Scripps' homes beginning in 1897 and that had created a gracious *allée* of palms that continued north and south of the site.

With the growth of the program and collection, the Board voted in 1964 to change the organization's name from the "Art Center" to the "La Jolla Museum of Art." Through the 1960s, under the direction of Donald J.

Brewer, and into the early 1970s, the exhibition program expanded its range from general art history to more contemporary art, showcasing artists such as Henry Moore (1963), Hans Hoffmann (1968), and Christo (1972), as well as local artists. Many art classes and workshops were offered on-site, and teachers included artists who were living and working in the area. Among those was the young John Baldessari, a native of National City, who taught summer school classes at the La Jolla Museum of Art before he moved to Los Angeles in 1970.

A view of the front of the La Jolla Museum of Art in 1968, looking north

A Museum for Contemporary Art

The Museum had come a long way from its early years, as subsequent directors and curators began collecting and exhibiting work of a broad national and international scope, eventually focusing exclusively on contemporary art. Discussions began in 1969 concerning this change of focus and, during the tenure of Director Thomas S. Tibbs, the Trustees adopted this policy: "The Museum will devote itself to Twentieth Century art with special emphasis on the art of today, including attention to the emerging artist. Practical considerations suggest that acquisitions by purchase should lay emphasis on the period from 1950 onward. The Museum will direct itself to the responsibility of being one among the several specialized museums in the San Diego area. At the same time, the Museum intends to achieve and maintain a significance, and to perform an educational function that will have more than local importance."[16]

In that same document, a definition of "contemporary art" was offered. "Contemporary Art is the art of our era. It is not 'contemporary' because it is created in the time in which we live, but because – in terms of the ideas that prompted it, its form, subject matter, or material – it investigates new areas and attempts in this search to change the way we see and perceive the world. It is the artist who defines what art is and who changes the boundaries of what art includes. It is impossible to determine whether the efforts of any contemporary artist will continue to have meaning in the future. But it is the excitement and challenge of a contemporary museum that

(left) Aerial view of the Museum of Contemporary Art, taken in 1988

it attempts to search out and present what, in its judgment, are important new concepts and directions in the area of art."[17]

Having set this strong institutional direction, the Trustees adopted the new name of "La Jolla Museum of Contemporary Art" in January 1971. Since then, the Museum has devoted itself wholly to the art of its times. In October 1992, to reinforce its regional role and commitment to the entire community, the name was modified by the Trustees to become the "Museum of Contemporary Art, San Diego" (MCA).

Since its birth as a community art center in 1941 and its later evolution into a professionally-run art museum, MCA has served the people of San Diego as a place for art exhibitions and art education. Each of its architectural modifications has accommodated steady growth in collections, programs and community use, with the Museum eventually gaining an international reputation for vanguard programming, a commitment to living artists, and unwavering support of the creative process. Beginning in the late 1960s, young artists (among them, John Baldessari, Chris Burden and Bruce Nauman) were given exhibition opportunities long before they became widely recognized, a programming predilection that is still a hallmark of MCA. The Museum pioneered the exhibition of installation art beginning in 1969, a time when such work was considered on the fringe of what was "acceptable" to show in a museum. Sherwood Auditorium has been an important local venue for performing arts as well as the Museum's own lectures, films, and educational programs.

Since the mid-1970s, MCA's reputation has grown dramatically. Today, it is recognized as one of only a handful of collecting institutions in the United States dedicated to contemporary art. In his ten years (1973-83) as director, Sebastian "Lefty" Adler was responsible for important acquisitions of Minimal art and an increasingly adventuresome exhibition program. He also oversaw a renovation that took place between 1976 and 1980, designed again by Robert Mosher. This project refined the renovations of two

decades earlier, consolidating the geometric "International Style" appearance by which the La Jolla Museum of Contemporary Art was known.

Since arriving as Director in September 1983, Hugh Davies has taken the Museum's acquisition and exhibition program in new directions, placed increased emphasis on education, scholarship and interpretation, and overseen an ambitious facility expansion and improvement in La Jolla and downtown San Diego. In a 1989 article in *The New York Times*, Davies was quoted: "We're not a passive repository for objects as some encyclopedic museums are, but an active laboratory for encouraging artistic experimentation and fostering creativity. We function as primary patrons for living artists."[18]

The collection now consists of some 3,000 works – painting, sculpture, works on paper, photography, video, and mixed-media works. MCA has special strengths in the areas of Minimal, Conceptual, and installation art as well as outstanding work by California artists, including many

(above) George Trakas, *Pacific Union*, 1987-88, Mixed media outdoor site installaiton, Museum purchase with matching funds from the National Endowment for the Arts, Art in Public Places Program

(left) A visitor in 1971 standing in Bruce Nauman's *Green Light Corridor*, 1970-71, wallboard, green fluorescent light fixtures, Collection Solomon R. Guggenheim Museum, New York, Panza Collection, Gift, 1992 (commissioned for and first exhibited at MCA in 1971)

Ellsworth Kelly, *Red Blue Green*, 1963, Oil on canvas, 83 5/8" x 135 7/8", Gift of Dr. and Mrs. Jack M. Farris

James Luna, *Half Indian/Half Mexican*, 1991, three black and white photographs by Richard A. Lou, 36" x 24" each, Museum purchase with funds from the Peter Norton Family Foundation Curator's Grant

TERMS MOST USEFUL IN DESCRIBING CREATIVE WORKS OF ART:

GIVE VISION	ENJOY	DISCIPLINE
DIRECTION	CHARM	DELICATE
FLAVOR	INFLUENCE	COMMAND ATTENTION
A NEW SLANT	INTEREST	EXALT
FORCE	DELIGHT	DEVELOP
UNIQUENESS	AROUSE	SATISFY
PERMANENCE	COMMUNICATE	BEAUTIFY
INSPIRATION	CULTIVATE	IDENTIFY
A GLOW	NURTURE	INSPIRE
MOTIVATION	PLAN INTELLIGENTLY	ORIGINATE
ENCHANTMENT	DETACH	CREATE
BLEND	TRANSFER	ASSOCIATE
ENLIGHTEN	CHALLENGE	CHERISH
INVIGORATE	ELEVATE	ALTER
ENTHRALL	SATIATE	REVISE
TAKE SERIOUSLY	IMPROVE	CRITICIZE
PRECISE CARE	VALUE	IMPRESS
OUT OF THE ORDINARY	FLAGRANCE	IMPART

John Baldessari, *Terms Most Useful in Describing Creative Works of Art*, 1966-68, Acrylic on canvas, 113 3/4" x 96", Gift of John Oldenkamp

from the San Diego region. Exhibitions are closely linked to the acquisitions program, and earn praise for their presentations of new work by vanguard artists. MCA curators organize many of the exhibitions presented and publish scholarly catalogues to accompany traveling shows, which are seen around the U.S. and abroad.

The Museum's national stature has been reflected in its accreditation by the American Association of Museums,[19] and a steady stream of grants from competitive federal government agencies, including the National Endowments for the Arts and Humanities and the Institute of Museum Services, and regional and national foundations such as The Pew Charitable Trusts, The James Irvine Foundation, the Lannan Foundation, and the Lila Wallace-Reader's Digest Fund.

GUARDED CONDITIONS

Lorna Simpson, *Guarded Conditions*, 1989, eighteen color Polaroid prints with twenty-one plastic plaques, plastic letters, overall dimensions: 91" x 131", Museum purchase/Contemporary Collectors Fund

One Museum, Two Locations

Beginning in 1986, MCA established a presence in downtown San Diego with a series of temporary "storefront" gallery spaces. But since 1993, the Museum has operated a permanent facility at America Plaza, an office and retail complex designed by architect Helmut Jahn. MCA Downtown, a free-standing 10,000 square-foot building adjacent to the San Diego Trolley line that runs through America Plaza, has become a cultural centerpiece of San Diego's urban area, and helps the Museum increase its outreach and community involvement. MCA's downtown presence will become even more important when the new San Diego Central Library, designed by Rob Wellington Quigley, opens next door in 2001.

The Museum building's configuration was the result of a unique artist/architect design team commissioned in 1992 to work within the Helmut Jahn shell. Artists Robert Irwin and Richard Fleischner and architect David Raphael Singer were engaged to design the simple yet effective interiors and, not surprisingly, given Irwin's involvement, MCA Downtown has unique qualities of light and space. The majority of MCA Downtown is devoted to galleries, thus increasing by 60 percent the total exhibition space in the two facilities available for programming.

The flagship La Jolla building is located in the "Cultural Zone" of historic buildings that was formed in 1987 by a City of San Diego planning ordinance to encompass the Museum, the Woman's Club, the La Jolla Recreation Center, The Bishop's School, St. James By-The-Sea Episcopal Church, and the La Jolla Presbyterian Church. In July 1994, after a decade of planning and fund-raising, the Museum broke ground on a $9.5 million renovation and expansion of the La Jolla site. The Philadelphia firm of Venturi, Scott Brown and Associates (VSBA) was selected to design the project.

Critic Paul Goldberger has stated that "Mr. Venturi and his wife and partner, Denise Scott Brown (co-author of much of his work since *Complexity and Contradiction in Architecture*), have together changed the way we see the world."[20] Widely regarded as one of most influential

(inset above) The new Santa Fe Depot in downtown San Diego, 1915; 78 years later, MCA's downtown museum would be built on the site of the vacant lot shown here, across from the depot

(right) MCA Downtown, 1993

(inset below) The San Diego Trolley station is adjacent to MCA Downtown

architectural firms of the late twentieth century, the Pritzker Prize-winning Venturi and Scott Brown have succeeded in revisiting the original Gill design in a sensitive, harmonious way. As Venturi himself has noted: "One can't 'compete' with the greatness of Gill, but it is our intention to respect the harmony of what can be considered his 'precinct' in La Jolla, through architectural additions that are analogous *and* contrasting."[21]

The VSBA design restores Gill's original Prospect Street facade of 1916, obscured since the late 1950s, and also provides dramatic new spaces – the covered Axline Court for public functions, reconfigured Edwards Garden, expanded Geisel Library, new Kockritz Education Center for teaching and learning, new cafe, larger bookstore, and new visitor orientation gallery. VSBA took a building that had many level changes, complex functional needs, and an eighty-year history of architectural modifications, and melded it into a rational, workable, elegant whole. Incorporated into the design were the existing Sherwood Auditorium and other elements of the building designed by Robert Mosher, as well as strong references to Irving Gill. The resulting "new" MCA is a harmonious enhancement to the historic architectural neighborhood that the Museum anchors.

Following the 1996 renovation, Goldberger praised VSBA's work in La Jolla: "The expanded museum is respectful of every piece of its complicated history, yet it has a strong and clear identity as a different building. It is a sharp and lively presence on the street, yet it is woven into the fabric of La Jolla with consummate delicacy and grace. The sense of balance between old and new, between object and context, is as subtle and as sure as anyone could ask for." In concluding his review of the building in *The New York Times*, he said: "Irving Gill is prime Venturi material: his architecture is simple, almost dumb at first glance, and wonderfully rich and deep the more you probe into it. Responding to a Gill masterwork that has had years of additions and subtractions, all within a busy urban context, is an architectural problem tailor-made for Robert Venturi. And the result is a good demonstration of

(above) Jonathan Borofsky's *Hammering Man at 3, 110, 527*, 1988, on view in the South Plaza, and his *Spinning Figure Eight With Three Chattering Men*, 1986, on view in the Danah Fayman Gallery of MCA Downtown

(top left) Works from the permanent collection in the second floor main gallery downtown

(bottom left) MCA Downtown, with Nancy Rubins' *Airplane Parts and Building, A Large Growth for San Diego*, 1994

what Mr. Venturi, often misunderstood as more of a theorist than a designer, has always been trying to make his architecture do."[22]

Venturi and Scott Brown have created a wonderful addition to San Diego's architectural landscape, a worthy "neighbor" to such landmarks as Louis Kahn's Salk Institute, just a few miles away from MCA. But most of all, the new building ensures that the Museum's programs will be available and accessible to generations of visitors into the next century, with collections, exhibitions, and educational functions enveloped in a structure equal to them in excellence and artistic importance.

(left) The Museum of Contemporary Art, San Diego, designed by Venturi, Scott Brown and Associates, 1996

(right) The restored Scripps House facade

One year after Hugh Davies arrived as Director in 1983, he was asked by the Trustees to, in a sense, act as a consultant and assess the Museum's strengths and weaknesses in preparation for a Trustee long-range planning retreat. The overriding conclusion of Davies' report was that the Museum needed more space to display its collections, needed to use its existing spaces more efficiently and effectively, and needed to enhance its ability to secure increased contributed and earned revenue. Most of all, the Museum deserved a building that took better advantage of its extraordinary site. The report became the touchstone for a January 1985 "colloquium" that generated extensive discussion and debate among the Board of Trustees. Eventually, by unanimous vote, the Board decided to engage an architect to develop a plan for the La Jolla facility.

The Architectural Commission

The Trustees felt it important to initiate a formal selection process for choosing the architectural firm that would expand and renovate the La Jolla building, and the process began in the Fall of 1985. Davies and then-Senior Curator Ronald J. Onorato worked closely with an Architectural Selection Committee composed of Trustees and community members, a number of whom traveled to other U.S. cities to see museums and new architecture by the leading candidates. The committee began with an initial list of forty firms – local, national, and international. This list was winnowed to four architects: Romaldo Giurgola, Mark Mack, Charles Moore, and Robert Venturi. Over a period of a month, each candidate came to La Jolla for a two-day visit to make formal and informal presentations to the Trustees and staff.

For the Museum, a key element of this interview process was a tour of the precinct of Gill buildings surrounding MCA, particularly the Recreation Center, the Woman's Club, and The Bishop's School. It is no coincidence that the winning architect, Venturi, and the first runner-up, Giurgola, had by far the most sympathetic response to the historic neighborhood in La Jolla. In fact, during his 1985 interview, Venturi almost reluctantly confessed to the committee that he felt the Museum should consider restoring the lost historic facade of Irving Gill's Scripps House.

MCA is at the apex of the street grid as it meets the curve of the coast on a diagonal, with an unusual and historic architectural uniformity in the surrounding Gill buildings to the east and the dramatic expanse of the Pacific Ocean to the west. The site clearly demanded an architect of experience and confidence to conjure with this potentially daunting duality, not to mention the jigsaw-

Through the Woman's Club arches, looking toward MCA across the street

(left) Denise Scott Brown and Robert Venturi, under the pergola at the La Jolla Woman's Club across from MCA

Looking south on Prospect Street, with St. James-By-The-Sea to the left

The courtyard of the La Jolla Woman's Club

puzzle-like existing building, which had accreted over time without benefit of a true master plan.

The committee's selection of Venturi, Scott Brown and Associates was confirmed by the full Board of Trustees, and a letter of invitation was sent in June 1986. Between MCA's selection of Venturi and his acceptance, the firm also won the prestigious commission of the new Sainsbury Wing from the National Gallery of Art in London. Venturi called Davies and asked if MCA wanted to reconsider, as the London project would take so much of VSBA's time and energy. However, the British museum's confirmation of MCA's instincts only steeled the Board's resolve to stick with their choice. The La Jolla client agreed to be patient in the years ahead. To his credit, Venturi was also patient with MCA, as the rigors of a lengthy local permitting process and the unpredictable fortunes of fund-raising delayed construction in La Jolla many years beyond the date originally envisioned.

Robert Venturi: Theorist and Practitioner

Venturi's contributions to architectural theory, most clearly embodied in his book, *Complexity and Contradiction in Architecture*,[23] as well as his experience in designing museums, made him an obvious choice for this contextually challenging commission in La Jolla. Perhaps the example of two buildings – one built in Ohio, one yet to be built in Texas – best illustrate Venturi's suitability for MCA's needs. The additions to the Allen Memorial Art Museum at Oberlin College in Ohio are much larger than the original building but are added in a

way that is respectfully off-center, contextual and deferential, while making a very strong design statement and a handsome partner to the existing historic building. The Oberlin commission is one of a succession of extraordinarily successful projects designed by VSBA for universities and colleges – a legacy of campus buildings which no other firm can match in the latter half of the twentieth century. The La Jolla project also drew on VSBA's experience in designing the Laguna Gloria Art Museum in Austin, Texas, an institution whose size and contemporary art mission closely mirrored MCA's. (This project, long on hold for lack of financing, is now back on schedule under the new institutional name of the Austin Museum of Art.)

Architectural Program

The next step in the process was to write the Architectural Program. Undertaken by Curator Lynda Forsha and Director Hugh Davies, this document was completed in 1986. It called for an additional 10,000 square feet of exhibition space and 2,000 square feet of art storage space as well as an enlarged library, the addition of a cafe, increased space for the bookstore, improvement of the auditorium, and creation of a gracious civic space in which people could congregate for the plethora of public events that are central to the functions and mission of any art museum.

In Venturi's first schematic plan (1987), which has remained essentially unchanged in the intervening decade, the new galleries – the "art portion" of the project – were

in a wing sited to the northwest, below the existing parking lot. Many of the other demands of the program, including revenue-generating areas such as bookstore, cafe, and auditorium, were captured around the new 5,000 square-foot entry court and in the Prospect Street facade. As Venturi originally posited, this now included a reconstruction of the original 1916 Irving Gill "Scripps House" facade. Due to a combination of local permitting problems, fund raising constrictions, and the irresistible offer of a handsome 10,000 square-foot downtown museum facility in 1992, the MCA Trustees reluctantly deferred construction of the new gallery wing, while enthusiastically seeking the attainable goal of creating a major new exhibition space in the heart of downtown San Diego.

The Trustees and staff are well aware that following this 1996 expansion and renovation, the La Jolla facility has a disproportionate ratio of support space to exhibition space. Only with the addition of the new northwest wing – comprising five galleries totaling some 10,000 square feet – will the Museum's Master Plan be complete. But with the continually challenging fund-raising climate for the arts, it seemed prudent to first build revenue-generating areas (which could make MCA more self-sufficient), while gaining 6,000 square feet of new exhibition space by pursuing the more cost-efficient downtown option. This goal was achieved in January 1993 with the opening of the permanent facility, MCA Downtown.

The Design Evolves over Time

Although from inception to completion it has taken more than a decade, the new La Jolla building has benefited from and drawn richly upon Robert Venturi's architectural lessons, not only of the still-unbuilt Laguna Gloria Art Museum but also from the Seattle Art Museum (commissioned and built between 1984 and 1991) and the National Gallery's Sainsbury Wing. For example, the choreography – in large and small steps both horizontal and vertical – introducing the curved stucco wall at the south end of the La Jolla facade echoes elements of the

Venturi's early sketch for the Museum project, 1988

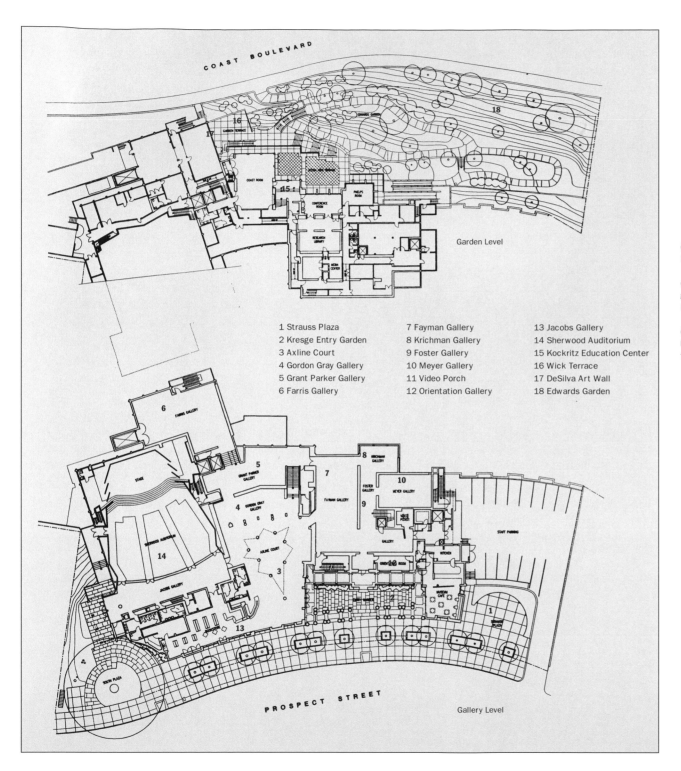

Garden Level

1 Strauss Plaza
2 Kresge Entry Garden
3 Axline Court
4 Gordon Gray Gallery
5 Grant Parker Gallery
6 Farris Gallery

7 Fayman Gallery
8 Krichman Gallery
9 Foster Gallery
10 Meyer Gallery
11 Video Porch
12 Orientation Gallery

13 Jacobs Gallery
14 Sherwood Auditorium
15 Kockritz Education Center
16 Wick Terrace
17 DeSilva Art Wall
18 Edwards Garden

Gallery Level

Floorplans of the renovated MCA, 1996

(top right) The starlight in La Jolla

(center) The arches over the grand staircase, Seattle Art Museum, VSBA, 1991

(bottom) The stairway and bifocal window leading west from the Axline Court, La Jolla

Sainsbury facade. Similarly, both museum projects revel in the perpendicular juncture of solid masonry wall meeting glass-and-metal curtain wall. In La Jolla, curtain walls bracket the reconstructed Gill house, which is set back from Venturi's arched facade. At the National Gallery, Venturi's masonry wall on Trafalgar Square turns back into the site to meet the glass-and-metal wall that runs the length of the grand staircase. This curtain wall ends at the masonry bridge, which is set back from the stone facade (like the Gill facade) and connects the new wing to the original Wilkins[24] building.

With the La Jolla project's protracted time-frame, there have been inevitable changes in Venturi's design over the years, many of them the result of strict discretionary planning dictates from the city of San Diego and other state and local governmental bodies. From his very first sketches, however, the Prospect Street side of the building featured the signature Gill arched windows, a contrapuntal rhythm of palm trees, a restoration of the Scripps House facade, and vine-covered pergolas.

If the facade was austere and "Gill-like," Venturi's proposed new dome surmounting the entry court reflected the more flamboyant influence of San Diego's other architectural "legend," Bertram Goodhue,[25] by surmounting the Museum's large congregational entry space with a dome, thereby identifying its civic function and complementing the domes and towers of neighboring churches and The Bishop's School. However, due to the intractable thirty-foot height limit in La Jolla, the resulting dome would have been too squat to be worthy of the name, and so Venturi countered with an oval drum containing the ribs or fins of a vestigial "dome" that had dropped, like a bowler hat into a hat box. This drum, with its clerestory glass windows and flat solid roof, is perhaps more technically a "lantern." Its oval shape, supported on paired columns, suggests the intimate seventeenth-century Roman chapels of Bernini and Borromini. Venturi's use of the oval to resolve and reconcile the existing trapezoidal walls that surround the space – now called the Axline Court in honor of the project's primary benefactors,

Jackie and Rea Axline – was reminiscent of Michelangelo's solution for the Capitoline Hill, which Venturi celebrated in a silver tray that supports the tea service he designed for Alessi, the Italian houseware manufacturer.

Perhaps the largest change in the La Jolla building between 1992 and 1995 was the evolution of the oval drum into an asymmetrical seven-pointed "starlight." Just as the original design for the facade with time had begun to appear too stuffy and repetitive, and hence gave way to the asymmetry of larger and smaller arches, so too the oval drum seemed too centered and perhaps funnel-like, given the overall proportions of the space it surmounted. The exuberance of the new star was probably triggered by Venturi's sketch of the multiple entry points of the Axline Court. These directional arrows, all centered under the dome, led to the stellar solution, which has the additional benefit of increasing the high-ceilinged portion of the Axline Court by 50 percent as well as commensurately augmenting the generous flood of natural light. He also reduced the number of supporting columns to seven and positioned them with unpredictable *élan*.

The respectful decorum and deference to Irving Gill in Venturi's exterior of the building is exuberantly countered by the starburst of energy – an architectural fanfare appropriate to a contemporary art museum – which greets the visitor upon entry. The design retains something of the history of its evolution, as the vestigial "fins" continue to serve their sound-proofing and deliberately decorative function. At night, the white neon (outlining the fins' individual wavelike profiles) functions as a cultural beacon.

The rectilinear geometry of the starlight is not only countered in the organic wave-profile of the fins, but also in the biomorphic gray-on-lighter-gray "spot" pattern of the terrazzo floor. Running diagonally through the Axline Court and leading the eye from the entry doors to the art in the galleries to the west, this dispersed pattern of repeated "puddles" was originally referred to by Venturi as "Dalmatian spots." In its final iteration, however, it

seems closer to the biomorphic abstract shapes of Jean Arp or perhaps to splotchy giant paw-prints. The Information Desk and its overhead ceiling in the Axline Court and the sides of the external stair to the Edwards Garden are the architect's most concise refrains of organic/geometric contrast.

In addition to the Axline Court, which both symbolically and functionally draws the disparate spaces of the building together, no feature changes the configuration or the use of the space more dramatically than the so-called "bifocal staircase," which leads down from the Axline Court to a series of terraces and the Edwards Garden to the west. The La Jolla design is based on a staircase in "High Hollow" (1914-16), the house that Philadelphia architect George Howe[26] built for himself in Chestnut Hill, Pennsylvania. At the top of that staircase, one looks straight ahead through a window to a distant view across a valley, while down the steps is a more intimate view of the garden below. In La Jolla, this bifocal vista is dramatically duplicated with ocean above and garden below.

In a fortuitous small echo of the Salk Institute, MCA visitors walking across the "bridge" spanning the stair are theatrically elevated and silhouetted against the window view of sky and sea in a way that suggests the performance quality of Louis Kahn's great court and framed westward vista. Standing in the Grant Parker Gallery on this bridge over the stair, one looks to the west through a cross-mullioned window, Venturi's quintessential signature, forward and out to the Pacific Rim. Turning back, the viewer sites through the star-lit Axline Court to a round-arched window that perfectly frames Gill's masterpiece across the street – the La Jolla Woman's Club. In architectural terms, one could not conceive a more succinctly poetic summary than this spatial haiku – a clear point in time poised and paused between past and future.

The Sainsbury Wing of the National Gallery of Art, London, designed by Venturi,
Scott Brown and Associates, 1991.

Sherwood Auditorium entrance, at the southeast corner of the Museum's Prospect Street facade

Details, Details

While Mies van der Rohe claims that "God is in the details," Venturi quips "Details wag de dog," and this Dalmatian-spotted edifice is replete with significant Venturi details. To mention only a few:

The overstuffed columns of the new Prospect Street pergola, in Venturi's words, are "analogous" to Gill rather than slavish copies. In fact, they are similar to the robust Doric pairs first used at the National Gallery which, like rolls on a baking tray, swell to the point of needing to be cut apart at the base. Compared to their domestic counterparts at the La Jolla Woman's Club across the street from MCA, their more substantial scale implies the substance and permanence one associates with civic structures.

To California eyes accustomed to the slenderest Neutra-like window mullions with barely sufficient metal to support the largest possible expanse of glass, one's first encounter with a three-and-a-half-inch Venturi mullion might feel it an unnecessarily overpowering frame and barrier to transparency. Yet familiarity breeds contentment, to the point of finding the mullions of modernism an anemic distraction in comparison to Venturi's substance.

A hallmark of Venturi is the design philosophy of overscaling select details to reinforce their symbolism beyond function, as well as the two-dimensional depiction of three-dimensional forms – found in his designs for chairs, his silver candlestick holder, or the fins in the Axline Court.

Finally, one might note the presence of the ubiquitous chair rail – Venturi's omnipresent through-line, the hallmark of any civilized room – which ironically and logically is deleted from the art spaces in La Jolla. Perhaps this all has something to do with Venturi's academically absent-minded and playfully perverse penchant for unbuttoned button-down shirts.

Fanfare

On one level, Robert Venturi sees the La Jolla museum building as a reflection of a kind of vernacular American house, with its formal front on Prospect Street and its casual, evolve-what-may backyard on Coast Boulevard. The various

Interior view, Sherwood Auditorium

The Coast Room (above) and Library (below), both part of the new Kockritz Education Center

appurtenances, protrusions, and additions to the rear attest to the progressive accumulation over time of successive new forms accommodating new functions. Venturi celebrates this contrast in the two facades. On the Coast Boulevard side, thanks to a dramatic elevation change at the rear of the building and the need to accommodate visitors in wheelchairs, the architect has created a very rich and elaborate composition. Curved and straight, rising and descending retaining walls, ramps and terraces begin to look like a compressed Cubist bas-relief when viewed from the street below – a bold, nautically-tinged composition perhaps by Léger, Ozenfant, or even Charles-Edouard Jeanneret.[27]

The Museum, from the very beginning of the design process, embraced the balance of Venturi's making a strong statement in the Axline Court, while keeping the extant galleries and the new wing art spaces appropriately neutral. We welcomed the resolute character of his memorable design for the entry space in the belief that visitors will not mistake MCA in La Jolla for one of the myriad of featureless museums of recent decades, in which architects puritanically purged personal statement in supposed deference to the art in the "white cubes" beyond the un-grand foyer. We believe, as does Venturi, that there is a place within a museum for architecture to assert itself – perhaps not to the full extent of Frank Lloyd Wright's Guggenheim, for example, but certainly more than one finds in the interiors of American museums since that brave moment. Just as Claes Oldenburg called for "art which does more than sit on its ass in a museum," we did not ask for a passive architectural repository and are delighted to have participated in the creation of a museum building that will actively engage and challenge both the visitors and the art it hosts in the years ahead.

As his clients for over ten years, we are enormously indebted to Robert Venturi for giving us his attention during this important decade of his career. Indeed, we revel in the fact that our building reflects the experience of an extraordinary architect at the height of his power and artistry. We have been privileged clients, and are now proud occupants.

The Axline Court, with Sol LeWitt's *Isometric Pyramid*, 1983, on view on the north wall

(top right) The Krichman Gallery, with works by Dennis Oppenheim and Vito Acconci on view during the inaugural exhibition in La Jolla, *Continuity & Contradiction: Selections from the Permanent Collection*, 1996
(bottom right) The Farris Gallery during the same exhibition

Design for the Museum of Contemporary Art, San Diego

Robert Venturi, FAIA, Hon. FRIBA
January 29, 1996

What a challenge! We had to demolish parts of, renovate parts of, restore parts of, and add to parts of the original complex of the Museum of Contemporary Art to make of the inside a whole which accommodates the extremely complex program of a modern museum, and to make of the outside a new civic building for the community.

On the outside we had also to acknowledge an urban context, rich and varied, and accommodate thereby a gently civic precinct of La Jolla. The Museum anchors this precinct, containing sublime historic buildings by Irving Gill in the front and a natural landscape in the back characterized by infinite space, that of the Pacific Ocean. On top of that, or within that, we had to excavate, expose and restore the facade of the Ellen Browning Scripps house entombed within the complex of 1960s extensions to the Museum, a house designed by Irving Gill that is an acknowledged masterpiece of American architecture in terms of its historical significance and aesthetic quality.

Of the new interior, we made a place that is essentially a setting for the exhibition of art, consisting of spaces neutral in their character and varied in their configurations that also accommodate flexibility for lighting and circulation. Occasional windows discreetly placed between the galleries facing the west permit occasional views of the garden in the foreground and the ocean beyond, whose momentary magical aspect is to complement the pervasive magic within the galleries of art.

But the museum program for today embraces significant spaces other than those dedicated to art – making up approximately two-thirds of the total area of the building and acknowledging educational, communal, social, administrative, storage, and mechanical and maintenance spaces including a library, auditorium, bookstore, and cafe with catering kitchen. And there is also here the central space that imagefully identifies this civic institution as a whole. This is the Axline Court whose architectural fanfare – spatial and ornamental – is appropriate just once within this otherwise recessive interior that is for cradling works of art.

On the outside, the architecture of this new building works to harmonize with that of the old buildings in front by means of analogy *and* contrast. Its symbolic and formal vocabulary is analogous to that of Gill's buildings via its abstract-cubist forms, multiple arched openings, and rhythmic columned pergola, while the larger scale of these forms along with the iconographic dimension within the design contrasts with that of Gill's building. This accommodation to context works to enhance the Museum's already beautiful setting by making it more of a whole. And it is the element of scale (large scale combined with small scale to accommodate perception by the individual up close and by the community at a distance) and the element of iconography, embracing symbolism and graphics, that make this building relevant for a civic institution in late-twentieth century San Diego. The facade is characterized also by its rhythmic composition, where the even rhythm of the line of trees along the sidewalk contrapuntally plays against the uneven rhythms and varying scales of the arches and columns. By its position right up to the sidewalk, this facade reflects the slight curve of Prospect Street and makes for an urban as well as a civic building.

A significant element of this civic-urban front facade is its signage, whose graphics are varied and very bold in their color, scale and lighting, and inherent to the composition. These graphic elements combine with the symbolic and representative forms described above to constitute the iconography that is essential to a late-twentieth-century building.

The relation of the newly revealed facade of the Scripps House to the newly designed facade of the whole is significant: the new facade works as a civic statement analogous to its context but it works also as a frame – as a context itself – to the earlier facade. And, as a frame, the new works to enhance the old by acknowledging its significance and reinforcing its character by creating contrast and encouraging comparison in scale, where the big civic scale of the new makes explicit the small residential scale of the old. And then there is the intimate quality of the forecourt as immediate context that the surrounding and enclosing new facade promotes. We hope the old facade becomes a precious jewel, protected via enclosure and enhanced via the space and scale of its new context.

The slight variations in the hues among the stucco facades of the complex are significant. The slightly pinkish-white hue of the original Gill facade (as well as the green of the window frames, mullions and door) corresponds to the original hue as interpreted from surface scrapings. The slightly grayish-white of the new front facade works subtly to reinforce the difference between the old and the new, and yet emphasize representation of the old in the new so the new appears almost like a black-and-white photograph. The same hue, slightly darker, is on the older 1960s forms of the building, protruding behind so they perceptually recede, and on the back facade as it recedes within the natural setting of the garden. The scenographic-representative quality of the new parts of the front facade is substantiated by the construction of their walls: that of conventional stucco-faced masonry rather than technologically progressive concrete slabs of which the walls of the original building are composed.

The rear facade of this complex consists mostly of the varied forms added in the 1960s, accommodating the idea, prevalent at the time, of designing from the inside out. We have enjoyed maintaining this picturesque effect of the design and enhancing thereby the contrast between the urban front (where you design from the outside in as well as vice versa) and the almost rural behind. Do we acknowledge a valid Queen Anne front and Mary Anne behind?

The landscape architectural element within this design is significant in the rear garden, a positive element of the architectural complex as a whole. Our main contributions to the composition here are the organic forms of the new stairs, ramps, retaining walls and paths that accommodate to the stylized natural landscape as well as to A.D.A. [the federal Americans with Disabilities Act] and fire code regulations. These organic forms work to contrast with the geometrical forms of the building itself.

Our most significant architectural contributions to the rear facade and its setting are the graphics that adorn the complex configuration of retaining walls and then the external mural. We are lucky that the Art Wall has a window in it and has an uneven border that perceptually integrate it with the building, and that the artworks can be changeable – the first being that by Ed Ruscha. The Art Wall adorns a face of the 1959 auditorium wing, perpendicular to the ocean at the scale of a billboard and at home at the edge of the Pacific Ocean. It finely, eloquently and iconographically expresses the contrast between the front and the back of this building that evolved over time between urban and rural, and local and universal contexts.

(top) The architect's mother, Vanna Venturi, in front of the house Robert Venturi designed for her in 1961

(bottom) The Scripps House designed by Irving Gill, 1916

Interview with Robert Venturi

Hugh M. Davies
Director, Museum of Contemporary Art,
San Diego

Ronald J. Onorato
Professor, Department of Art, University of
Rhode Island, and former Senior Curator at
MCA (1985-88)

July 13, 1994, La Jolla, California

HMD: I wanted to start by asking you to talk a bit about our setting and the opportunities afforded by east and west, by Irving Gill, and the ocean and the town of La Jolla.

RV: I love the question because I love the setting. And the setting had lots to do with the design. We have been interested in the idea of context for a long time – it is now a kind of cliché among architects, but it is a valid consideration.

The essential responsibility we had in designing this museum – or the extension of it or the renovation and restoration of parts of it – was to make the museum work well inside. But very close in importance was accommodating the context. And the context here is absolutely fascinating because there is the well-known and very much appreciated Gill "precinct," as I call it. Here, I refer to the context toward the east – the front of the museum which connects with the town. How we connect here is very important. But there is also, fascinatingly, the other part of the context: the Pacific Ocean. One context is urban and relatively small in scale while the other, toward the west, is vast – the world's largest body of water.

This museum, in accordance with its contrasting contexts, is very different in front from what it is in back. This had a significant effect on its architecture, because there were the functional/programmatic needs in between these layers of back and front that had to be accommodated to make a good and workable museum inside. And so there are the contradictory responsibilities inside and out, front and back.

HMD: Could you talk about your response to Gill and your history with him? We know you've been coming here to San Diego over the years to visit his buildings.

RV: Well, Irving Gill has always fascinated me. I'm not an expert on Gill. I'm not an historian. I've spent some time thinking about Gill as a practicing architect, and he's an enigma to me. I looked up the word the other day to see if there were a noun, to see if there would be a wonderful word like "*enigmat*," a person who was enigmatic. But the darn dictionary did not produce one. Nevertheless, Gill is, for me, an "enigmat" because he is many things at once. You have to associate his work over the whole length of his career, including Spanish Revival, Arts and Crafts, California Mission Style, and then

Abstract Cubist Modern.

With Gill as context, we found we could achieve a harmony with the complex of four Gill buildings that face our site. They had a direct influence on our architecture. We decided that we would achieve harmony with these buildings mostly by means of analogy, but via contrast as well.

So the outside wall of the front of our complex is composed in the manner of Gill, but in some ways it is significantly different from Gill. The scale is bigger – this is the late twentieth century and this is a civic building that connects with the region and not just with the local area of a small town as did the older institutional buildings. So we are like Gill in using severe whitish forms, but the scale of our openings is bigger. We are unlike Gill in making our building essentially a facade on the front. You don't read it as a three-dimensional form. It is frankly an urban facade.

It's doing a job on the outside that contrasts with what's going on in the inside. So there is a feeling of layering – of contradictory layering. Gill made buildings that were essentially three-dimensional with four sides, in a world of

The La Jolla Museum of Contemporary Art, 1981

The new Museum, 1996

lots of space. Ironically, we are not compelled in the late twentieth century to exploit what was, in the early twentieth century, advanced technology inherent in reinforced concrete bearing walls; so our walls – for the sake of economy – can be old-fashioned stuccoed masonry.

Of course, there is much richness within our facade as a whole, revealing the sublime Scripps House facade. Here, the facade of the relatively big-scale civic museum diminishes into a more domestic scale as it approaches the Scripps House. And then the Gill-like pergola within this facade on Prospect Street works to soften the bigger scale of the new facade, where it meets the old one. So, in another way, the residential scale of the Gill facade is acknowledged along with the larger scale. I think we have created a good context within a context, where the new building declines and inflects as it meets the old, and the old building is seen behind a screen, while the whole of the front acknowledges the neighborhood.

The back of the museum is kind of like the traditional American house, where there's a sort of *ell* and where all hell can break loose. A number of functional, pragmatic wings protrude, deriving from additions from different eras. And then there is also the iconographic dimension manifest in the "Art Wall." All this creates a different kind of beauty from that of the abstract and serene front. Our designing here, from the inside out, represents a Modernist mode and a good one. And here, we don't have to accommodate urban spatial demands. We are connecting with the immediate

small scale of the residential part of town at the shore, but also to the vast ocean. So our big-scale "Art Wall" and our small-scale forms work to accommodate big and little contextual elements.

RJO: You brought up some ideas that might relate to the new wing you designed for the Allen Memorial Art Museum [Oberlin, Ohio] and the Sainsbury Wing of the National Gallery of Art [London]. They're both works that you did related to existing buildings. Are they different from or similar to what you've done here? Was your process different?

RV: I think the process was quite similar, although each of the buildings is very different. If you accommodate and build

for context on the outside, that means you don't have a universalist vocabulary appropriate for all. There's nothing wrong with such an approach – Renaissance architecture promoted a universalist ideal – but such an approach is not necessarily appropriate for the multi-cultural world we're in. This is a big subject. Essentially the buildings you mentioned – the Oberlin Museum and the extension to the National Gallery in London – are very different from each other partly because of their very different contexts, but there is a similarity because they are buildings – or wings, if you will – that inflect toward and are harmonious with the old. In the case of the Sainsbury Wing, it is mostly analogous, but with very extreme exceptions. At

Oberlin, we were employing analogy and maybe contrast in equal amounts that makes for a *tour de force*.

HMD: There's something of a contrast between the restrained facade of our museum and what happens in the interior. It's a bit of a surprise when you get inside, something I find very exciting about the design. Perhaps you could talk about the change of aesthetic that occurs when you cross the threshold.

RV: Well, that was fun – we were having fun in a responsible way. A building that is a museum has to accommodate inside context as well as outside context. It has to work as background for art but at the same time it has to be artful in itself, artful and

(left) Rear view of the Museum, taken from the cliff below

On view in the Edwards Garden in 1996: Edward Ruscha's *Brave Men Run in My Family*, 1995-96, Mauro Staccioli's *Untitled*, 1996, and Nina Levy's *Infantile Tree Ornaments*, 1996

Paired columns in the Italian painting galleries, National Gallery of Art, London, designed by VSBA, 1991

Detail, entry pergola at the Museum of Contemporary Art, San Diego, 1996

imageful. It has to be recessive and positive. So it has to be an artful building that is a context for other people's art inside. And that is the case with a majority of this museum's interior spaces – the most important spaces, the galleries. The gallery spaces should be generically neutral and recessive and capable of being used in different ways; they should be perceptually if not spatially flexible.

However, there can be a certain moment when a museum, which is also a civic building, can engage in some architectural fanfare. What we're doing is being responsible on the outside concerning context and responsible on the inside concerning art, but we can engage flair at a certain point. A museum today allows for that, because it is a place not only for exhibiting art, but also a place for civic occasions. It must promote civic gesture and symbolism – and be able to accommodate education, administration, sales, dining, and so forth.

So as you leave the outside and enter into the Axline Court, you find a place which is a civic, festive place where lots of different things can happen. Most of the time it can be an exhibition space, too. It is wonderful to have exhibitions near the entrance so you know you're in an art museum as soon as you enter. But it is also an immediate place that maintains its own character – this mainly via the lantern in the ceiling. That lantern is set back and works as a kind of a star-shaped dome, not apparent from the outside – at least from close-up.

So as you enter, it is a surprise when you find most of the fanfare in the upper part of the space. This is the place where we can do our "thing." But remember: we are appropriately accommodating to Gill on one side, to the community and to nature on other sides – and to art elsewhere inside.

HMD: In the Axline Court, there is something I've found interesting. What was the evolution from the original drum – which was elliptical, oval, and very central as was the pattern on the floor – to this very eccentric, almost freehand star-shaped form, seven-pointed and independent?

RV: I don't have much rationale. I think what we're saying is that the original building and its additions are basically geometrically and rationally based. They are subdued for the reasons I've mentioned – context outside, art inside – but there might be one moment for flair that is in some ways irrational, that's expressionistic so as to make the rest more wonderful via contrast. When you leave the court, you go into reticent architecture, against which the varying kinds of art will be displayed over decades. So I think the Axline Court is a kind of irrational moment involving fanfare that makes more vivid the rationality of the rest of the building. It's "Hey, let's dance a little jig here. We can do this, and this is part of life." I guess there's a kind of fun in the fact that the shape and plan of the lantern is star-like and angular, and then the fins which catch the light as it comes in the windows are the opposite – organic and curvy.

A view of the starlight in the Axline Court, with the La Jolla Woman's Club visible through the windows and Alexis Smith's *Men Seldom Make Passes At Girls Who Wear Glasses*, 1985, on view

I think there's a moment for whimsy, even in architecture, although there is less than in other media, where you don't have to spend so much money to keep the rain out and all the other things which make architecture such a highly responsible kind of art.

Here in La Jolla, it is interesting that the approaches to this building on the east side, the main facade, are diverse and interesting. I love the fact that the facade curves, because that's again acknowledging an exterior urban quality – the curve of the street. So you generally approach it obliquely, but you also approach it head-on, from Silverado Street. That's the time outside that you can see the lantern from a distance and that identifies this building, from a distance, within the "Gill precinct."

HMD: I was delighted when I saw the "starburst" lantern and the terrazzo spots, the wonderful wave patterns on the reception desk and the outer stairwell. Could you talk a bit more about how those elements evolved? Some of them are recognized from earlier phases, but then there are many surprises, too.

RV: I am usually analytical, and I think I can justify what we do in our designs. The question concerning the waves – I haven't really discovered where they come from, we don't use them elsewhere, but I like them. We have many different styles of working because of our contextual bent. I guess we use the waves to contrast vividly with the geometrical configurations of Gill that we are otherwise accommodating analogously.

We needed a dash of contrast. And we don't like doing a building whose parts are unified in an obvious way. Our buildings are not like Frank Lloyd Wright's, whom I admire as perhaps the greatest American architect. But his buildings have an enormous consistency and motival unity which you admire rather like that of Rococo architecture – Wright would be horrified by that analogy! – with its *rocaille* all over. His consistency exists in the furniture, in patterns for the lady-of-the-house's skirts, as well as all over outside and inside, and including the andirons.

So we like it that our compositions do not make an easy totality. The waviness in the Axline Court used contrasts with the geometry of the architecture because that makes sense in our complex ethos.

I also have no rationale for the pattern on the Axline Court floor, except to say that it's saying "this is a place for pattern" and it is similarly contrasting with the whole. When there is art on the walls in the Axline Court, this floor might make it a little harder for the curators; but it is only relatively recently that museums promoted hyper-neutral settings for the exhibition of art. Anyway, I think there is a need for these touches of fanfare as you enter a museum. Now, one can go too far with that, and I think many museums of the last decades contain over-blown architectural expression. By the time you get to the art, you're perceptually worn out. The art then becomes an anticlimax. So ours must be a modest element, high up in the ceiling at the beginning of your experience in the building.

HMD: It seems to me that a great mistake a lot of museum clients make is trying to create a neutral container, because then the building relates to no time and serves really no art.

RV: It's a very interesting point, and one to which there's no easy answer. The idea is fascinating – that you have to be positive and of your time but also not intrusive. Here in La Jolla, we do that in different ways and with different intensities in different parts of the building. There is the issue of not being distracted when you're looking at the art, yet, at the same time, there should be moments when you are distracted, in the sense that you have a kind of intermission, as you do in the art of the theater. You can't sit in a theater for two hours straight during a play; you need the relief of an intermission once in a while – which then makes the magic more wonderful when you return to it.

So here in La Jolla, you have occasional chances to look outside at views and thereby remember where you are. You are in the world of art in the galleries, where you can focus. But then, as you pass to another gallery, you can look outside and you can exclaim as you observe the Pacific. You can't look out at the town of La Jolla from any gallery, but you can remember where you are generally in the world, and compare it to the wonderful world you have just been in – the world of art which you're lucky to be going back into. All of this is important in the sequential perception of things while you're in the museum.

RJO: Denise Scott Brown's input and influence are enormous, especially from the urban design side. I remember when we first looked around this site, she had very visceral responses to the configuration of the streets, the way Silverado comes right down perpendicular to the side and then Prospect Street undulates around. I wonder if you might talk about her role?

RV: Her role is most significant and very varied. Besides designers, architects today have to be salesmen, showmen, psychiatrists, businessmen, lawyers, socialites, travelers, all these things at once. So we both spend a lot of time doing all that. We no longer have a business partner, so we're doing all that intensively.

In design, Denise is involved crucially. There's very much the urban design dimension that specifically connects with work that our office does in cities and in master planning for institutions. She is also significantly important as a critic during the process of design, architectural and urban. T.S. Elliot said 90 percent of creativity involves criticism: standing back and criticizing what you're doing and then coming back and redoing it. So her role as a critic – an understanding, perceptive, and creative critic – is essential.

RJO: Could you talk a bit about the exterior wall of the Farris Gallery – the "Art Wall"?

RV: This is an idea that came together as we all discussed the character of the west exterior – that of making one of the big walls a kind of "mural" – and thereby

Inaugural exhibition, Part I, 1996, *Continuity & Contradiction: Selections from the Permanent Collection:* (top left) Jacobs Gallery, (top right) Farris Gallery

(bottom) Inaugural exhibition, Part II, 1996, *Blurring the Boundaries: Installation Art, 1970-1996,* Fayman Gallery

accommodating an iconographic dimension within the architecture, appropriate as you connect art and architecture literally in a museum.

I should back up and mention that one of the general difficulties about doing museums is that you can't have many windows. Some clients require no windows at all. In galleries in our museum in Seattle, for instance, they said "no windows" – they had very high standards for preservation and the effects of natural light on art. But in other places, we can admit some natural light as we can here – very carefully modulated for the sake of preserving the artworks.

Without any windows, a museum can often look awkward on the outside. It can even look ominous: the buildings you associate with no windows are jails and forts. So here in La Jolla there is a very big wing with no windows – Sherwood Auditorium and the existing Farris Gallery connected to it. We love the idea of having a big and reasonably bold work of art on one of those exterior walls – a work that will change over time. And we are so happy that the first artist will be Edward Ruscha,[28] whose art we have admired and adored for a long time.

Another reason we like this "Art Wall" is because it makes the difference between the museum's front and back more explicit and eloquent. The front is very much "Gill-ian" in its severe abstraction. It certainly has no ornament or any kind of iconography within it. So I love the richness that will derive from its back

containing an iconographic element – almost billboard-like in its boldness as it can be read from a distance in its context. This is an element that says something about art in an explicit way – eloquently saying something about what's going on inside. We love this element, which promotes contrast and richness as it juxtaposes the iconographic and the abstract. Here we are being different from, yet respective toward, Irving Gill.

HMD: You, more than just about any other architect, have designed museums in the twentieth century, and ours is a museum specifically for contemporary art. In some ways, I think that is a more difficult charge than to design for a general historic museum, where you have a much better sense of what's going to be contained within – with a fixed collection such as the National Gallery's. There, one couldn't ask for a better situation in which to view the art in that collection. But here, we can't tell you what the art is going to be in this collection in years to come.

RV: I agree that is a relevant issue. The National Gallery extension, as you said, involved an especially unusual case where there is an established collection that varies only slightly over decades. You don't acquire a new Raphael very often. So it represents a static and specific situation. You accommodate the art there with a setting that should be more, let's say, art object-specific, and it is appropriate there to do that.

The American museum is generally one where there is much more flexibility, where collections are growing, or where

Museum Bookstore

Museum Cafe

there are many traveling exhibitions. I remember when I was in college, I very often went to The Museum of Modern Art in New York. I think that was probably the first museum that established the essential "generic loft space" – neutral and white, flexible in terms of spatial configuration, character, and light. MOMA, let's say, institutionalized the idea of the neutral white space, the flexible environment for art. And it was a good idea. The furthest extreme can be the "black box" theater approach where the individual curator totally manipulates loft space for different styles or different periods in the evolution of art and the museum. Here, it's the curator's job more than the architect's to create architectural setting.

I think that here in La Jolla, we worked between two extremes. You say this place has an established identity, but you also make the place as generically simple and flexible as possible. You make the natural lighting and the opportunity for changing artificial lighting work well.

So here, we've been not at all original. We have said, "Yes, we want to use the ongoing American tradition for museums," which is neutral exhibition spaces that curators can change over time. I don't think the walls should always be white. But, on the other hand, that tradition is generally a good one. Probably most of the time they should be. So essentially what we're trying to do is make this place as "generically loft-like" and therefore as flexible as possible in terms of spatial divisions and the lighting.

HMD: Sort of Mies-ian...[29]

RV: Yes and no, I would say: Mies did promote what could be called generic loft space – incidentally and ironically derived from the vernacular American industrial loft – but his aesthetic with its accompanying abstract-minimalist dimension would not permit aesthetic clutter and the kind of richness derived from clutter. Frank Lloyd Wright, by the way, accommodated an aesthetic clutter but one totally controlled by this architect who verbally preached Emersonian individualism – one that was strictly motival, as I've said, and thereby, in the end, as aesthetically imposing and pure as Mies'. Now, we're in an age of authentic clutter. We're back to a kind of Victorian clutter that Mies and Wright were reacting against.

HMD: So it hasn't swung back to Mies. It's swung to a different sensibility. What makes your firm so relevant today in the sense that Wright is no longer in sync with our time?

RV: I hope that what we're doing is relevant for today. But we're still, I'm happy to say, controversial. When you talk to people about us, we can be thought of as either old young Turks or just old Turks. I hate to criticize what's going on today because I don't want to be in the position of a sour old man – but a lot of what's going on involves a kind of expressionist revival of universalist Modernism in old-fashioned industrial drag, whose hype compositions end up being trite. This should be a time when we glory in richness and ambiguity and the coming

together of many things in validly dissonant ways.

I think a lot of the industrial elements employed today, ironically as ornament, are not appropriate. The industrial vocabulary that was discovered as appropriate for architecture in the early twentieth century is now an historical vocabulary. The technology and therefore the imagery of the Industrial Revolution is as historical as that of the Renaissance that re-employed Roman Classical orders. So this whole idea of referring to the technology essentially of the Eiffel Tower – which was very exciting in the old days – and applying it as ornament, is irrelevant and ironical.

Of course the technology of today is electronic, and this is going to be the time for re-employing iconography by employing electronic iconography, not abstract-industrial form that is defined by the light and the shadow of the sun, in the way Greek buildings were. We ought to go a little beyond the Classical Greeks now, so our buildings can be defined more by iconographic imagery than by form in light, industrial form or any other kind. We are more and more interested in an architecture that's based less on form and more on symbol, less on industrial technology and more on an electronic technology, less on expressionist architecture and more on generic architecture.

But it is true that this idea of re-acknowledging symbolism and signs goes way back in our work. And a lot of our designs in the past – such as the Football

Hall of Fame and our thinking involving Las Vegas – does connect, the more I consider it, with historic iconography. The use of generic architecture as a basis for symbolic, iconographic elements is significant now that an expressionistic industrial vocabulary is boring and minimalist abstract expressionism in architecture is boring, too. You no longer can love architecture for its pure and formal expression.

HMD: What of the issue of permanence? What troubles me a little bit about the "decorated shed" idea is its ephemerality. I like the fact is that the images could change, but the fact is that the billboard itself could fall over.

RV: I can understand this, especially if you love Chartres, for example, which is still there essentially as it was. But if you're an older architect like me, you go back to the buildings you did in your early days and they're shabby. That's partly because they're not being maintained very well for lack of operating budgets and because your construction budgets have been loaded 40 percent for mechanical equipment, not leaving much left for finish materials. For these reasons our buildings tend to be ephemeral, even when we pretend they aren't. You look at any early Modern building; it's often in a shabbier state than a building built five hundred years ago.

But the idea of employing ephemeral iconography is very appealing in some ways. Generally, the iconography and theological content that was established in churches, such as in the mosaic murals of

Ravenna, were eternal. And that goes for the iconography of Fascist architecture. Permanent messages can be bad as well as good.

Changeability, of course, is different from what you were referring to – which is impermanence of the fabric. That is something that is a modern characteristic, and is a shame. But the idea of change-ability can also be wonderful. In the past, when buildings were adapted and changed, that was usually negative – although not always; there are a lot of great Rococo churches whose *rocaille* surfaces contain a Romanesque structure below. Now, maybe modification can be built-in and can be positive in its effect. It's an interesting subject. It's a difficult subject, but I think more and more we're going to find that our architecture is ephemeral. It's no longer going to be, in terms of its use or its fabric, as permanent as even a Roman ruin. That's sad but we have to face it. And maybe there can be something positive about it.

HMD: In the art world, there are all these discussions about virtual reality and computers and the information revolution. Will the original work of art no longer be exciting enough to compel people to make the effort to come to a museum, when they can sit at home and see the art on a computer screen? And maybe architecture is going the same way?

RV: It is. And you in the art world are talking about it, are facing it positively, more than we architects are. We're more naïve and we continue to wallow in a

sentimental industrial ethos and ignore the relevance of iconographic media.

HMD: To get back to Irving Gill...

RV: An interesting question to me is "Did Loos know Gill?" Irving Gill evolved just before Adolph Loos.[30] Probably no one will ever know, but it is significant that Loos derives from a kind of ideological stance: that simplicity and lack of ornament are superior; that ornament is evil. We all know the famous quotation that equates "crime" and "ornament." So his was a kind of moral stance that can be dangerous in art.

But our Irving Gill was someone whose work evolved differently – pragmatically, possibly out of an existing regional style of architecture, out of Spanish Colonial. But he's also out of the Arts and Crafts Movement and the Mission Style. And then he had written about his interest in technological and maintenance efficiency and economy. These ideas embraced social dimensions – you could build more cheaply, you could build more effective buildings for low-income people. All this pragmatic richness, for me, promotes wonderful aesthetic tension. You look at those Gill arches and can ask: are those arches historicist-revival or modernist functional? But with Loos, his minimalist abstraction is unambiguously based on a kind of moralist consistency.

So, to me, Irving Gill remains the enigmatic artist whose art can evolve from and represent many things at once. Gill, to me, is intensely contradictory when you look at his work. The evolution of his work

is just fascinating, as one sees in the wonderful book by Bruce Kamerling.[31]

HMD: It's great the way Gill says that nature will decorate.

RV: Yes, that's also captivating and interesting and relevant and original – as in a bas-relief of vines on a wall!

HMD: Gill would probably say that ornament is grime. It would collect dirt.

RJO: Bob, you really do see the influence of Arts and Crafts that strongly in Gill?

RV: Yes – especially in his early work – but also in the quality of the detailing of his windows.

HMD: What I find ironic but endearing is the fact that your place in history is much greater than Gill's, and yet you have such deference for your predecessor on this project.

RV: I would not agree with you at all on that. History is tricky. I'm old enough to have seen the fickleness of the cycles of taste. But Denise Scott Brown and I are in a difficult position because we're mannerist architects, and that's perversely hard to understand.

Notes

1 Schaelchlin, Patricia A., *La Jolla: The Story of a Community, 1887-1987* (La Jolla: Friends of the La Jolla Library, 1988).

2 Venturi, Robert, and Denise Scott Brown, *Learning from Las Vegas* (Cambridge: The MIT Press, 1972, rev. 1977).

3 "One Hundred Years of Significant Buildings: 9: Houses Since 1907," *Architectural Record* (Feb. 1957): 199-206.

4 Irving John Gill, born in New York, 1870; practiced in California 1893 to 1936; died in San Diego, 1936. See Kamerling, Bruce, *Irving J. Gill, Architect* (San Diego: San Diego Historical Society, 1993).

5 "One Hundred Years of Significant Buildings: 9: Houses Since 1907," see Hugh Sinclair Morrison, "Ellen Scripps House, La Jolla, 1917 [sic], Irving Gill (Tied for ninth)," 204. Morrison mentions architects Bernard Maybeck, 1862-1957; Charles Sumner Greene 1868-1957 and Henry Mather Greene, 1870-1954; Henry Hobson Richardson,1838-1887; Louis Sullivan 1856-1924; Frank Lloyd Wright, 1867-1959; Claude-Nicolas Ledoux, 1736-1806; Charles-Edouard Jeanneret, known as "Le Corbusier," 1887-1965.

6 Gill quoted in James Britton, "Art of the City," *San Diego Magazine* (June 1957): 40-41,60.

7 Gill, Irving J., "The Home of the Future: The New Architecture of the West: Small Homes for a Great Country," *The Craftsman*, (May 1916): 147-148.

8 McCoy, Esther, *Five California Architects* (New York: Reinhold Publishing, 1960).

9 Adams, R., "The Simple Cube with Creamy Walls," *The Reader*, San Diego, June 16, 1994.

10 Casserly, Jack, *Scripps: The Divided Dynasty*, (New York: Donald I. Fine, Inc., 1993).

11 Kate Sessions,1857-1940.

12 Gill, "The Home of the Future: The New Architecture of the West: Small Homes for a Great Country," 140, 142-147.

13 "Art Center Fund Grows To $11,817.50," *La Jolla Journal*, Thursday, March 13, 1941.

14 Robert Mosher (b. 1920; practiced in San Diego, 1946-1993), Roy Drew (b.1913; practicing in San Diego 1948 - present). The firm of Mosher & Drew was founded in 1948; Robert Mosher was the principal architect on the La Jolla renovations of the Museum. In 1969, the firm became Mosher, Drew & Watson; since 1979, it has been Mosher Drew Watson & Ferguson.

15 Mosher, Robert, *Oral History Interview* by Cordelia Ryan, January 30, 1993, Museum of Contemporary Art, San Diego.

16 Trustee policy, La Jolla Museum of Contemporary Art, revised December 21, 1971.

17 Written by LJMCA Curator Jay Belloli and incorporated as Trustee policy, La Jolla Museum of Contemporary Art, 1971.

18 Glueck, Grace, "Two Small Museums Grow with the Economy," *The New York Times*, February 6, 1989: B1+.

19 MCA's accreditation citation, American Association of Museums, 1987, Henry Hopkins and Constance Glenn, reviewers: "We find this to be one of the finest institutions of its type in this country. It serves its population with distinction; its collections are focused, important to the region and the field, and well-managed; its setting is idyllic; its programs are of the highest quality and directed by a talented staff; and its financial management is sound."

20 Goldberger, Paul, *The New York Times*, April 14, 1991.

21 Venturi, Robert, Lecture, Museum of Contemporary Art, San Diego, May 1988.

22 Goldberger, Paul, "Refashioning the Old, With All Due Respect," *The New York Times*, May 5, 1996.

23 Venturi, Robert, *Complexity and Contradiction in Architecture*, The Museum of Modern Art Papers on Architecture (New York: The Museum of Modern Art, 1962; reprinted 1966).

24 William Wilkins, 1778-1839.

25 Bertram Goodhue, 1869-1924.

26 George Howe, 1886-1955.

27 Fernand Léger, 1881-1955; Amédée Ozenfant, 1886-1966; Charles-Edouard Jeanneret ("Le Corbusier"), 1887-1965.

28 Edward Ruscha (1936 -), *Brave Men Run In My Family*, commissioned by MCA and installed on the DeSilva Art Wall at MCA in La Jolla, March 1996.

29 Ludwig Mies van der Rohe, 1887-1969.

30 Adolph Loos, 1870-1938.

31 Kamerling, *Irving J. Gill, Architect* (San Diego: San Diego Historical Society, 1993).

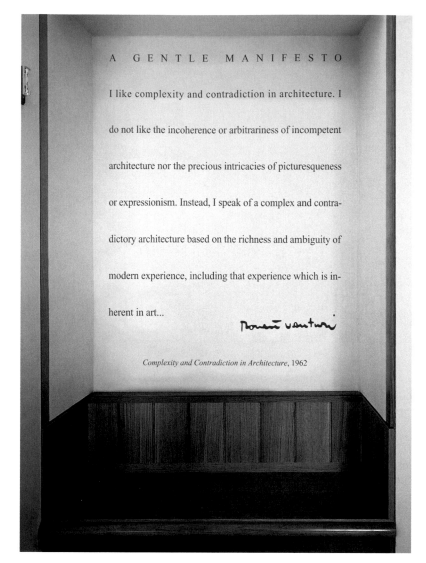

A GENTLE MANIFESTO

I like complexity and contradiction in architecture. I do not like the incoherence or arbitrariness of incompetent architecture nor the precious intricacies of picturesqueness or expressionism. Instead, I speak of a complex and contradictory architecture based on the richness and ambiguity of modern experience, including that experience which is inherent in art...

Complexity and Contradiction in Architecture, 1962

Inset bench located inside the Axline Court